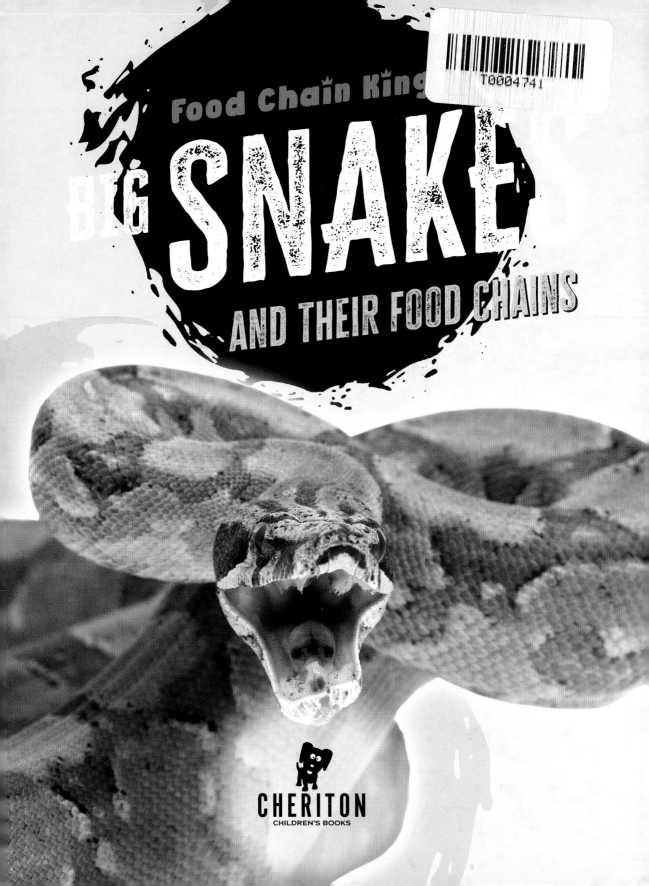

Food Chain Kings

BIG SNAKES

AND THEIR FOOD CHAINS

CHERITON
CHILDREN'S BOOKS

Published in 2023 by **Cheriton Children's Books**
1 Bank Drive West, Shrewsbury, Shropshire, SY3 9DJ, UK

© 2023 Cheriton Children's Books

First Edition

Author: Katherine Eason
Designer: Paul Myerscough
Editor: Elise Harding
Proofreader: Hayley Bennett
Illustrator: Martyn Cain

Picture credits: Cover: Shutterstock/Karel Bartik; Inside: p1: Shutterstock/Fivespots; p4: Shutterstock/Vadim Petrakov; p5: Shutterstock/Reptiles4all; p6: Shutterstock/ Sandra Matic; p7: Shutterstock/Ralfa Padantya; pp8-9: Shutterstock/Karel Bartik; p10: Shutterstock/Egoreichenkov Evgenii; p11: Shutterstock/Dirk Ercken; p12: Shutterstock/K Hanley/CHDPhoto; p13: Shutterstock/Reptiles4all; pp14-15: Shutterstock/Stephanie Periquet; p16: Shutterstock/Gulliver20; p17: Shutterstock/ Ohmega1982; p18: Shutterstock/Heiko Kiera; p19: Shutterstock/Objectsforall; p20: Shutterstock/DWI Putra Stock; p21: Shutterstock/Roy Palmer; p22: Shutterstock/Dr Morley Read; p23t: Shutterstock/Audrey Snider-Bell; p23b: Dreamstime/Picstudio; p24: Shutterstock/Paul Tessier; p25: Shutterstock/Dr Morley Read; pp26-27: Shutterstock/ Michael Park Art; p28: Shutterstock/Fivespots; p29: Shutterstock/Nick Greaves; p30: Shutterstock/Rogerio Peccioli; p31: Shutterstock/Cynoclub; pp32-33: AdobeStock/ Mathieu; p34: Wikimedia Commons/Nobu Tamura; p35: Shutterstock/Michael Rosskothen; pp36-37: Shutterstock/Daniel Eskridge; p38: Shutterstock/Rich Carey; p39: Shutterstock/Mitchell Kranz; p40: Shutterstock/Howard Sandler; p41: Shutterstock/ Elliotte Rusty Harold; pp42-43: AdobeStock/Alejandro.

Printed in China

Please visit our website,
www.cheritonchildrensbooks.com
to see more of our high-quality books.

CONTENTS

CHAPTER 1

KILLER KINGS

Many of the world's **habitats** are home to snakes, one of the most successful **predators** on Earth. Snakes are awesome hunters that are equipped to track down **prey** with lethal precision. And of these great hunters, boas and pythons are the biggest.
Both are impressive snakes that kill their prey by squeezing it to death.

Some boas, such as anacondas, can be huge. This anaconda measured around 20 feet (6 m) long.

Chain Champs

Big snakes are part of both land and water food chains. A food chain is a series of animals and plants that are connected because they depend on each other for food. Each animal in a food chain is linked to the animals and plants below it. Big snakes are at the top of many food chains because these fierce predators hunt other animals, which in turn feed on smaller animals or plants. Plants are at the bottom of most food chains.

Not on the Menu

Many people are often terrified of big snakes such as pythons and boas, and in rare cases, some pythons have killed and eaten humans. However, this is very unusual, and these giant hunters rely on prey that is more naturally found in their **environment**.

Pythons, such as this Burmese python, are strong, long snakes with powerful bodies.

Links in the Chain

Food chains are made up of producers, consumers, and decomposers. Animals that eat other animals are called secondary consumers, and the plant-eating animals they eat are called primary consumers. The plants that primary consumers eat are called producers. Decomposers break down the waste produced by consumers and producers.

Deadly but Different

While boas and pythons look similar, they have some important differences. Boas live mainly in the western part of the world, in Central and South America. Some do live in Africa and on islands such as Madagascar, Fiji, and Reunion Island. Pythons are mainly found in Africa, Asia, and Australia.

Similar but Not the Same

Boas and pythons also have some physical differences. Compared with pythons, boas have fewer bones in their heads and fewer teeth. Boas tend to be colored brown, tan, red, or gray, and have different patterns. Pythons usually have solid colors and only have diamond patterns.

Although boas have fewer teeth than pythons in their jaws, they are no less spectacular when they open wide!

BABY HUNTERS

Another big difference between boas and pythons is in the way they reproduce, or create young. Baby boa snakes are born live. Pythons lay eggs, and baby snakes hatch from them. Baby snakes are known as hatchlings.

This baby python is hatching from its egg.

Long or Heavy

Boas also tend to be smaller than pythons—most measure between 4–12 feet (1–4 m) long, although the green anaconda is a boa that can grow more than 20 feet (6 m) in length. Pythons can often grow more than 20 feet (6 m) long. However, the boas have the edge when it comes to weight—the giant in their family, the green anaconda, is the heaviest snake in the world.

HELLO WORLD!

BIG BOA HUNTER

The boa constrictor is one of the most impressive of boa snakes. One reason why it is at the top of its food chain and can kill and eat large prey is its size. Most boa constrictors grow to about 10 feet (3 m) long and weigh over 100 pounds (45 kg).

Boa constrictors slither along the ground and up trees, eating almost anything they can catch. A boa lunges at its victim, and seizes it with its sharp teeth. Then, the snake wraps its body around the prey and squeezes it until it stops breathing. The giant snake then swallows the animal whole.

*Super-hunter boas have **flexible** bodies and very sharp teeth. This boa is swallowing a rat head-first!*

Squeeze and Eat

Where in the World?

Central
America

South
America

The boa constrictor is found in Central and South America. It is the ruler of the **rain forest**, but the mighty snake also lives in **deserts, grasslands,** and fields. It particularly loves rain forests, because in these hot and damp places there are many plants to hide among and a lot of animals to hunt. A boa keeps still in its hiding place and lies in wait for prey, such as a passing rat. When the animal scuttles by, the snake lunges out and grabs its meal.

People used to think that boas killed their prey by **suffocating** it, but scientists have discovered that the animal dies because as it is squeezed by the snake, its blood cannot move around its body. That stops blood reaching the heart, which kills the prey.

IN THE FOOD CHAIN

Being big and heavy means boa constrictors have the strength and weight to bring down large animals, such as wild pigs. The snakes also eat rats, birds, and monkeys.

Boa constrictor food chain

WILD PIG

BOA
CONSTRICTOR

EGGS

CHAPTER 2

DESIGNED TO KILL

Almost everything about big snakes makes them quite perfect predators. They are armed with ultra-**efficient** senses that help them seek out prey that other hunters may not be able to detect. And when they do find their prey, these deadly killers seize it with incredible speed and impressive power.

Victim Vibrations

Big snakes do not have ears on the outside of their bodies, so they do not hear sounds in the way a human does. However, they can sense when prey is moving nearby by "feeling" the **vibrations** the animal's movements make in the ground. Snakes have stomachs that are very sensitive to movement—they can actually feel vibrations in their bellies! If a snake feels a lot of shaking of the ground, it knows that big prey is nearby. If only small vibrations are felt, the predator can tell that just little animals are in the area.

Both boas and pythons can feel even the slightest vibrations in the ground and air —leading them straight to prey.

Killer Night Vision

Snakes such as boas can see well at night because they have straight, upright pupils that can get bigger in dim light. This lets in as much light as possible to help the snakes see prey that come out at night—even from a distance. The vertical pupils may also look like blades of grass to any potential prey, helping the snakes hide until the time is right to lunge and seize the animal.

JAWS NOT JUST FOR EATING

A snake can even feel vibrations in the air in its jawbones, which helps it detect flying prey such as birds. Sounds are picked up in the snake's jawbones, and then travel to the cochlea. This is a body part that helps an animal hear. There, **nerves** pick up the sound signals and send the information to the brain.

A boa's pupils are designed to let in as much light as possible to help the animal spot prey.

Super Senses

A snake uses a very smart trick to make sure it finds all possible prey. It uses its tongue to "smell" other animals. As it moves through the darkness, the snake sticks out its forked tongue to pick up scents and tastes in the air. This guides the hunter to its next meal.

Prey Tracker

When the snake pulls its tongue back into its mouth, it passes the scents and tastes it has picked up onto a patch on the roof of its mouth called the Jacobson organ. This organ passes messages to the brain, which figures out what the scents and tastes are. The snake then knows what type of prey is there and how to find it.

Heat-sensing pits are super senses that help big snakes hunt in the dark.

FLICK AND FIND

As a snake slithers along, it flicks its tongue in and out of its mouth about once every second, and even faster sometimes. The forked tongue means that smells can be gathered from two different points, at the same time. As a result, information about where prey may be is given to the snake's brain in record time, leaving prey animals little time to escape the awesome predator.

A forked tongue with two tips helps snakes figure out which direction a smell is coming from.

Heat of the Hunt

Boas and pythons also have small pits on the front of their heads that act as heat sensors. The pits sense heat given off by a nearby animal's body to help the snakes figure out what and where it is. Scientists now believe that the snakes can hunt with deadly accuracy at night because they convert, or change, the heat from nearby prey into electrical signals that lead them directly to the animal.

MONSTER HUNTER

The African rock python is a monster of a snake. It can grow to a length of 16 feet (4.8 m) and weigh up to 250 pounds (113 kg).

Like other large snakes, African rock pythons lie in wait for their prey. When a tasty animal comes near, the snake lunges forward and seizes it. The large, muscular snake then wraps its hefty body around its prey and squeezes it until it stops moving. The animal is so big and powerful that it has even been known to hunt and eat prey as large and powerful as crocodiles!

An African rock python rests after it has eaten a huge meal. It can take months for this giant snake to digest large prey.

Africa

Cub Killer

The African rock python lives throughout most of **sub-Saharan** Africa. The area it is found in reaches from Senegal and Ethiopia through Somalia, Namibia, and South Africa. The snake lives in many different habitats, including forest, grassland, and semidesert. It is also found near **swamps**, lakes, and rivers, because it is a good swimmer.

African rock pythons eat many different types of animals, from rats, monkeys, and birds through bats, lizards, and deer. They have also been known to hunt and eat the cubs, or babies, of another top predator—the big cat. Leopard and lion cubs have all been made a meal of by this giant snake predator. The African rock python has been able to **adapt** to changes in its environment, and as farmers have entered its habitat, the snake has survived. It hides out in fields of crops and is known to feast on farm animals.

IN THE FOOD CHAIN

African rock pythons eat large prey if they find it, including antelopes and warthogs. The huge snakes also hunt chickens, goats, and dogs, which makes them unpopular with local farmers.

African rock python food chain

MONKEY

LIZARD

AFRICAN ROCK PYTHON

CHAPTER 3

KILLER BODIES

All snakes have long bodies and no arms or legs. Instead of walking, they slide across the ground or swim through water. Snakes have dry skin that is covered with hard scales, which overlap each other like the tiles on a roof.

Large pythons can wrap their coils around prey as big as antelope to squeeze the animal to death.

Snakes are covered in scales. Scales are thick pieces of dead skin that protect the soft flesh beneath them.

Jab or Squeeze

Although some snakes jab their fangs into animals to **inject** them with venom, or poison, boas and pythons do not. These big snakes only use their sharp teeth to grip prey, and rely on their enormous bulk to literally squeeze the life out of the animal.

Twist and Crush

Snakes are vertebrates, which are animals with a backbone. The backbone is made up of pieces of bone called vertebrae. Humans have just 33 vertebrae, but some snakes have more than 200 vertebrae, which makes them very flexible. Boa constrictors have very flexible backbones that are connected to around 400 ribs, and some **species** of python have up to 600 vertebrae! Having many vertebrae allows the giant snakes to twist and coil their bodies around their prey.

COLD-BLOODED KILLERS

Snakes are cold-blooded. That means they cannot control their own body temperature, so their bodies are usually only as hot or cold as their surroundings. That is why these big snakes can be seen lying in the sun, to warm their bodies, or hiding under rocks or bushes, to seek out shade if they need to cool down.

17

Pythons, such as this Burmese python, and boas can swim quickly through water.

Designed to Hunt

Big snakes can move across ground, climb trees, and even swim to hunt for prey. The snakes have also been known to hang from branches, holding on with just their powerful tails, while they lunge into the air to grab animals.

Pushy Predator

A snake moves in a very special way—by using its muscles to push or pull against rough surfaces. First, a snake grabs the ground with scales on its tail, then pushes against the earth to move itself forward. As it does so, it folds and unfolds its body, moving in a wavy pattern. A snake can also travel with its body straight by moving the skin of its belly forward and then pulling itself along, a little like an earthworm.

Master Mover

To climb trees, a big snake such as a python or a boa bunches up its body in horizontal loops, moves its head forward, and then straightens out its body again. To swim, it curves and turns its body from left to right, making "S" shapes again and again. Each time the snake turns, it pushes against the water behind it to move itself forward.

Snakes make an "S" shape as they move across the ground.

PYTHON POWER

Although pythons are mainly **freshwater** swimmers, some have been found swimming in salt water in ocean areas around the coast. Some pythons can stay underwater for up to 30 minutes. These muscular super-killers may lie in wait at the water's edge, then use their enormous power and strength to lunge out at animals that come to drink.

Cunning Constrictors

Pythons and boas look similar because they have both **evolved** to develop physical characteristics that help them hunt in their environments. For example, boas and pythons that live in trees have eyes on the sides of their heads, which help them spot prey all around them. Whereas boas and pythons that spend their time in water have eyes on the top of their heads, so they can see prey above the water as they lurk just below the surface.

Hidden Killers

The colors and patterns on the boa constrictor's back help it catch prey. Most boa constrictors are colored brown, cream, or gray, and have oval, diamond, or circular patterns across their backs. This **camouflages** the snakes against their background, so prey cannot see them.

Pythons that live in forests are colored to match their environment, such as this green tree python.

PSST!— OVER HERE!

Some boas are brown to match their habitat.

Changed to Kill

Scientists call the way in which two species adapt to their environments in similar ways "convergent evolution." The animals have grown to look alike because their bodies changed in similar ways to better suit their similar environments. The changes in both boas and pythons have made them more effective hunters in their habitats.

Hiding Hunters

The snakes' coloring is also adapted to suit their environments, helping them hide from prey in the habitat they live in. The snakes that live in forest areas are colored to blend in with the green trees around them, whereas snakes that live in swamps or other wetland areas are colored to blend in with their watery backdrops. Although boa constrictors do not often go into water, when they do, their coloring and pattern help camouflage them in the brown-green waters of rivers and lakes. This helps them sneak up on prey animals that feed at the water's edge.

Sneaky Hunters

Boas and pythons are big, heavy snakes, so they cannot move as quickly as many of the fast-moving prey they hunt. Unlike some predators, big snakes do not chase after their prey. These huge hunters instead must rely on smart tricks to catch their kills.

Ambush Attack

One trick that big snakes use is to **ambush** their prey. The snakes are ideally camouflaged to hide from prey animals, so they may lie in wait for them to pass, all the while hidden perfectly against their backgrounds. When the prey is near, the snakes lunge and grab it.

Boas remain still and hidden until prey comes close. Then they strike!

SWING AND SNAP!

Sometimes, smart snake predators also lie in wait at cave openings and in trees to catch birds and bats that fly past. They wrap their tail around a branch to hold on to it. Then they swing out the rest of their body to catch animals that fly past in their hungry jaws!

This snake is patiently waiting to catch prey that may fly past it.

Setting a Trap

Big snakes also set traps for prey. Sometimes, a snake finds a prey animal's burrow, which is a hole or series of holes an animal makes underground to live in. The snake then waits by the entrance for the animal to come out. And when it does …. snap and squeeze, the snake makes a meal of the unsuspecting victim! Boa constrictors also lurk by water, waiting for animals to come to drink. When the animals come near, the boas grab them and squeeze them tight.

Boas grab bats in the air as the bats fly by, searching for food.

Egg Warming

Female pythons are oviparous, which means they lay eggs. After the female has laid the eggs, she keeps them warm until the baby snakes within them are ready to **hatch**. Keeping eggs warm while the babies grow inside them is called incubating. Once the eggs are laid, it takes between 50–60 days for the babies to hatch. When the snakes are about to hatch from the eggs, they change appearance. They look less round and are saggy.

Boa Babies

Unlike python mothers, female boa constrictors incubate eggs inside their bodies—the eggs grow inside the mothers' bodies, with the babies inside them. When the babies are fully grown, the eggs break open. The mother snakes then give birth to up to 60 live baby snakes at a time. The babies are up to 2 feet (0.6 m) long and fully developed when they are born, so they can slither and slide across the ground.

BORN TO KILL

Baby big snakes start life eating smaller prey, such as mice and rats. As they get older and bigger, they need more meat to fill them up. They then begin to hunt and kill bigger and bigger prey to feed their growing bodies.

Small but Deadly

Most big snakes leave their young straight after giving birth, so baby snakes start to live alone within minutes of being born. They slither off into the undergrowth to hide from birds, wild pigs, and other predators that might try and catch them while they are small. The baby snakes are not entirely helpless, though. They are born knowing how to hunt and soon start to catch their food.

A python mother keeps her eggs warm until it is time for the baby snakes to hatch.

Young snakes climb trees more often than adults to find and catch food.

SEE ME CLIMB!

25

INVADING HUNTER

The Burmese python is a huge snake, with a body as thick as a telephone pole! Females can grow to 23 feet (7 m) long and weigh up to 200 pounds (90 kg).

Burmese pythons are one of the biggest snakes in the world, but they are best known for the way they catch their food. These massive snakes have sharp, backward-pointing teeth. The snakes use the teeth to hook onto their prey and grip it. Then the giant killers coil their massive bodies around the victim, squeezing and squeezing, until the prey animal breathes its last breath. Finally, the snake opens its mouth wide to swallow its lifeless prey.

This is the skull of a Burmese python. The snake can open its mouth wide enough to swallow animals that are five times the size of its own head!

Where in the World?

North America

United States

Snake Invader

The Burmese python is naturally found in **marshes** in southeast Asia. However, in recent years it has been found in the swamps of Florida. That is because people have kept the huge snake as a pet, and the animal either escaped into the wild or was released there by owners who found this monster pet too difficult to handle. In Florida, the snake is an invasive species, which means it is an animal not naturally found in an environment. Invasive species are a problem because they disrupt natural food chains and **ecosystems**. Large snakes such as the Burmese python will prey upon animals in the swamps, and eat too many of them, which harms the natural food chains in the swamp areas.

To try and track down the giant snake, scientists have planted male "scout" snakes and released them into the swamps to find female pythons to **breed** with. The scientists track the males as they travel toward breeding grounds, and the females there. The females can then be removed so that they do not breed and introduce more pythons to the swamplands.

IN THE FOOD CHAIN

Burmese pythons eat mainly small **mammals** and birds, but if they grow large enough, the snakes sniff out bigger prey such as pigs and goats. In the Everglades, invasive Burmese pythons have even been known to attack and eat alligators!

Burmese python food chain

BURMESE PYTHON

GOAT

SHRUB

CHAPTER 4

DEADLY ATTACK

A big snake may be patient while it waits for prey to come near, but when the moment comes to strike, the snake attacks with deadly speed and a sharp aim. It darts forward quickly, opening its mouth wide as it closes in. Before the animal realizes what is happening, the snake digs its sharp teeth into its body.

Boa constrictors use their teeth to catch large and small prey.

I'M A FANG-TASTIC HUNTER!

Crushing Coils

Next, the giant snake quickly wraps its flexible, muscular body around and around its prey. If the prey is small, the snake pulls it into the coils. If the prey is larger, the snake moves itself forward onto the prey, wrapping the coils further around it. The snake then tightens the coils and squeezes and squeezes.

In a Heartbeat

As the giant snake squeezes, it looks for signs that the prey's blood flow has been cut off and cannot reach the **vital organs**. When the prey's heart stops beating, and the animal also stops breathing, the predator senses it. The snake then relaxes its deadly coils.

This python is killing a monkey by squeezing it to death.

HOOKED BY A HUNTER

A boa constrictor has small, sharp teeth that curve backward. Once dug into prey, the teeth act like hooks and stop the prey from wriggling out of the snake's mouth. If the teeth become damaged and fall out, new ones grow in their place.

This python is eating a teiu lizard head-first, after suffocating it and breaking its bones.

Open Wide!

As soon as the snake has caught and killed its prey, it starts to eat it. Unlike other predatory animals that have **limbs**, snakes don't have hands or feet with which to hold their food! Nor do they have teeth that can cut into flesh to tear it into pieces. These predators have no choice but to swallow their food whole.

Head-First Hunter

Snakes have stretchy **ligaments** that connect the bones in their jaws. This allows them to open their mouths very wide, which is why they can swallow animals that are bigger than they are—and these super predators tend to eat their prey head-first to make the process a little easier!

STILL BREATHING

You may wonder how a big snake can still breathe when its mouth is filled by a large animal that it is slowly swallowing. It can do so because a special tube in the bottom of its mouth remains open on one side so the snake can take in air.

Squeeze and Push

Once the snake has wrapped its jaws around its meal, it pushes it into its stomach. With smaller prey such as a rat, a snake uses muscles inside its body to squeeze the prey down through the throat and into the stomach. With larger prey such as a deer, the snake uses bones in its head to move forward onto the prey, and thereby push it into its body.

Feast and Fast

In the stomach, the animal is broken down by strong acids. However, because a snake cannot partly break down its food by chewing it before swallowing, its stomach must work extra hard. It can take a long time for a snake to digest a meal, which is one of the reasons why this big predator may not eat again for several weeks.

GOING, GOING, GONE!

Muscles in a python's throat squeeze hard to pull its prey down into its stomach.

31

GIANT HUNTER

Anacondas are the heaviest snakes in the world and are also one of the longest—females can grow up to 30 feet (10 m) long, which is longer than a bus! Anacondas belong to the boa family, and the green anaconda is the biggest of all. It can weigh up to 550 pounds (227 kg).

Green anacondas are water-loving hunters. They are so huge that they must spend most of their time in water, where it is easier for the snakes to move. For that reason, they are sometimes called water boas. Anacondas hide just below the surface of the water, waiting for prey to come near. Their nostrils are positioned directly on top of the nose, so they can stay hidden beneath water while still being able to breathe.

South America

Brazil

This is an illustration of a green anaconda. The snakes are big and bulky on land, so move slowly across the ground.

Brazilian Beast

The green anaconda lives in South America. It is found in the Amazon Rain Forest and also in the wetlands of Brazil. The anaconda is happiest in water and is found in the marshes, swamps, and streams of the Amazon area.

The green anaconda is a truly magnificent monster of a snake, however, even this giant predator is threatened by another animal—humans. People who live in the Amazon are frightened of the snake because they fear it will attack them. Although attacks on humans are incredibly rare, when they have happened, they have instilled terror into people, who hunt down the snakes to prevent further tragedies.

The snake is also hunted for its skin, which is turned into decorative objects and leather. Another threat to the snake is the destruction of its habitat—year on year, more of the precious rain forest is destroyed. As the rain forest disappears, so too do the prey animals the green anaconda relies on. Both its habitat and its food chain are under threat.

IN THE FOOD CHAIN

Anacondas are huge, so they can eat very big prey. The snakes feed on birds, turtles, capybara, and wild pigs. They sometimes eat other predators too, such as jaguars and caiman!

Green anaconda food chain

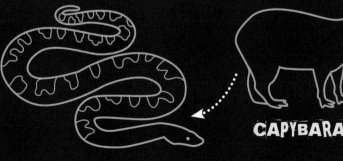

ANACONDA

CAPYBARA

SUGAR CANE

CHAPTER 5

PAST PREDATORS

Snakes have been slithering on Earth since about 145–65 million years ago. Some scientists believe snakes came from land-living creatures, while others believe they evolved from animals that lived in water.

Super Sea Snake

The biggest sea snake believed to have ever lived was *Palaeophis Colossaeus*. This mega sea snake lived millions of years ago, and died out about 33 million years ago. It was up to 30 feet (39 m) long, and probably ate animals as big as whale calves. The snake swam in constantly warm seas, which is why it grew so large. Unlike modern snakes, it did not experience cold, so did not need to rest and conserve, or hold on to, energy in the cold. Instead, *Palaeophis Colossaeus* was warm much of the time, so could keep moving, hunting, feeding—and growing bigger.

*Huge **prehistoric** snakes such as Palaeophis would have dominated the waters that they swam in.*

I WENT DOWN IN HISS-TORY!

In 2002, scientists discovered the skeleton of the biggest snake to have ever lived—Titanoboa.

Giant on Land

As its name suggests, *Gigantophis* was a truly gigantic snake! It measured about 33 feet (10 m) long, from the tip of its head to the tip of its tail. It lived about 40 million years ago in an area of land that is now North Africa, swimming in swamps. Like the super-big anacondas of modern times, the bulky snake would have been more comfortable in water than on land. This super snake probably ate large mammals, including an ancient relative of modern-day elephants.

WONAMBI WONDER

Wonambi grew to 18 feet (5 m) long and weighed up to 100 pounds (45 kg). It lived about 2 million years ago, in Australia. Like modern pythons and boas, the snake hunted by curling its huge body around its prey and slowing squeezing it to death. However, unlike pythons and boas, Wonambi could not open its mouth wide, so probably fed only on small wallabies and kangaroos.

MEGA HUNTER

When the huge **fossil** of *Titanoboa* was discovered in 2002, it made news worldwide—as the biggest snake to have ever lived. It measured an incredible 42 feet (13 m) long, or more, and weighed about 2,500 pounds (1,135 kg). Put simply, it was massive and even longer than a school bus!

Titanoboa was probably an ambush expert that lay in wait for passing prey, then struck at speed. It would have hooked prey with its sharp teeth, then delivered an enormous crushing hug with its muscular coils that were capable of constricting, or squeezing, with a force of 400 pounds per square inch!

This illustration shows Titanoboa *attacking a crocodile!*

Where in the World?

Colombia

South America

Killer of the Swamp

Titanoboa lived in the swampy rain forests of an area that is now South America. In 2009, fossils of 28 *Titanoboa* were found in Colombia, along with fossils of giant turtles and enormous crocodiles.

Titanoboa lived about 60 million years ago, soon after the **extinction** of the dinosaurs. It probably spent most of its time in water, because it would have been too big to move around on land—much like the enormous green anaconda of today.

Earth was much warmer during the time of *Titanoboa*, which is why it was probably able to grow so big. Like *Palaeophis Colossaeus*, the warm waters in which *Titanoboa* lived meant that the snake could keep active, regularly hunting, feeding, and growing ever-bigger. The snake probably died out when Earth's **climate** changed, becoming colder.

IN THE FOOD CHAIN

Titanoboa probably fed mainly on fish, but may have also eaten much bigger and more dangerous prey, such as alligators. It could probably have swallowed a large prehistoric crocodile whole!

Titanoboa *food chain*

TITANOBOA

CROCODILE

WATER PLANT

FISH

CHAPTER 6

FOOD CHAIN FIGHT

The main dangers that boas and pythons and the prey they eat face are from people. Their habitats are being destroyed and the land is being cleared for farms, highways, and towns. This leaves the snakes and their prey without a place to live.

Snake Terror

When farmers live close to snake habitats, they kill the snakes because they eat the farmers' chickens. Some people also kill the snakes out of fear. They are scared of attacks from pythons, because sometimes people have been harmed or even eaten by the giant snakes. And although boas cannot eat humans, people fear them because they can deliver a painful bite.

NOT PERFECT PETS

People also catch or breed big snakes to sell them as pets. It is shocking to think that up to 1 million snakes are bought and sold every year, and from 1975 through 2018, more than 4 million pythons alone were bought and sold. Not all of the snakes are sold as pets, but those that are can be very difficult to keep. Big snakes are not meant to be pets—their place is in the wild, not in someone's home.

Hunted Hunters

People also hunt big snakes to sell their skins and meat. In some places, snake body parts are sold and used in medicines or for religious purposes. The animals are also threatened by changes to their habitats. As more and more wild places are cleared for farmland, the giant snakes have less space in which to hunt for food. And as roads are built in the places in which they live, the snakes sometimes are hit and killed by passing vehicles.

Precious snake habitats are often cleared to make room for farmland or other human activities, such as mining.

Some people hunt boa constrictors and sell their skins to make goods such as belts, boots, and purses.

Survive and Thrive

What happens when snakes disappear from the top of the food chain? You might think that the animals below them would thrive if snakes disappeared. This is what people once thought, too, but they were wrong. When snakes disappear, animals lower down the food chain also suffer.

It is important that boas remain at the top of their food chain for the health of other animals and people, too.

Helpful Hunters

If there were no big snakes at the top of a food chain, the whole ecosystem would change. Every living thing in the rain forest depends upon one another for survival. If one animal is removed, every other animal and plant is then affected. Predators help maintain the balance of plants and animals within a habitat, which keeps it healthy.

I'M A HELPFUL HUNTER!

RAT CATCHER

Rats gnaw through wood, plastic, and cardboard to steal food. Their dirty paws and droppings **contaminate** stored food, and they carry fleas that spread disease. Boa constrictors are such great rat hunters that in parts of South America, people keep the snakes to catch rats.

Boa Control

An example of how important big snakes are to their food chain can be seen in the boa constrictor. These snakes eat rats and opossums, and help keep their numbers down. Without boas, the number of rats and opossums would very quickly grow. If there were many more of these animals, they would become pests in some areas. That is why we need big snakes such as boas and pythons to stay at the top of their food chains.

Like rats, opossums can be a pest that eats garbage and spreads disease. A healthy boa population can help keep the number of opossums under control.

HEAVYWEIGHT HUNTER

A reticulated python can grow to a length of 29 feet (9 m) and has a weight of up to 595 pounds (269 kg)! It's called a reticulated python because of the mixed pattern of its brownish-yellow and black scales. The female python is usually larger than the male.

The reticulated python opens its jaws wide to swallow its prey whole.

Like all constrictors, the reticulated python is a heavyweight hunter. It is perfectly camouflaged to hide among the rain forests in which it lives. There, it lies in wait for its prey to pass by, then seizes the victim in its jaws. The python then wraps its bulky body around the animal and squeezes tight. The food is then swallowed with one giant gulp.

Super Swimmer

Reticulated pythons live mainly in the rain forests and marshes of southeast Asia. Like the Burmese python, reticulated pythons have also been found in the Everglades of Florida. They too are an invasive species, and harm the natural food chains and ecosystems of the swamps.

The pythons can also be found in woodlands and grasslands, but they are often found near water such as near rivers and lakes. People have even found the snakes in sewers in Singapore, Indonesia, and Borneo. The reticulated python is an amazing swimmer, and people have even seen the snake swimming far out at sea. In fact, the snake is such as strong swimmer that it has swum from the **mainland** to islands to find a new home in which to live and hunt.

IN THE FOOD CHAIN

The reticulated python mainly eats different mammals and birds. The snake may also feed on rats, bats, monkeys, deer, and pigs, among other animals. People also report that the snake snatches pet dogs and cats when they stray into villages and cities.

Reticulated python food chain

RETICULATED PYTHON

BAT

MOTH

ULTIMATE KILLER!

WHO IS THE ULTIMATE KILLER KING OF THE BIG SNAKE KINGDOM TODAY? CHECK OUT THE FOOD CHAIN FACTS BELOW, THEN YOU DECIDE!

BOA CONSTRICTOR

AVERAGE LENGTH	10 feet (3 m)
AVERAGE WEIGHT	100 pounds (45 kg)
FOOD CHAIN SNACK	mouse
FOOD CHAIN FEAST	wild pig
KILLER BLOW	is a sneaky ambush hunter that strikes at speed

AFRICAN ROCK PYTHON

AVERAGE LENGTH	16 feet (5 m)
AVERAGE WEIGHT	121 pounds (55 kg)
FOOD CHAIN SNACK	bat or rat
FOOD CHAIN FEAST	crocodile
KILLER BLOW	is an aggressive hunter that has adapted to its changing world

BURMESE PYTHON

AVERAGE LENGTH	21 feet (6.4 m) (females)
AVERAGE WEIGHT	80-200 pounds (36-90 kg)
FOOD CHAIN SNACK	bird
FOOD CHAIN FEAST	pig (or alligator in the Everglades!)
KILLER BLOW	can open jaws wide to swallow prey five times bigger than its head

GREEN ANACONDA

AVERAGE LENGTH	17 feet (5 m)
AVERAGE WEIGHT	66-154 pounds (30-70 kg)
FOOD CHAIN SNACK	turtle
FOOD CHAIN FEAST	caiman
KILLER BLOW	the biggest of all snakes, so can eat the biggest prey

RETICULATED PYTHON

AVERAGE LENGTH	16-20 feet (4.5-6 m)
AVERAGE WEIGHT	375 pounds (170 kg)
FOOD CHAIN SNACK	rat
FOOD CHAIN FEAST	wild pig
KILLER BLOW	an adaptive hunter that can make a city its home

GLOSSARY

adapt change to better suit the environment

ambush a surprise attack from a hidden place

breed to mate and then produce babies

camouflages hides against a background

climate the usual temperature and weather

contaminate to make dirty or harm

deserts places that receive little or no rainfall

ecosystems environments and the plants and animals that live in them. All of the things in an ecosystem depend on each other to survive

efficient works well and without wasting energy

environment the natural world or the natural place in which a plant or animal lives

evolved changed over time to better suit its environment

extinction the process of dying out

flexible easily bends

fossil the hardened remains of a dead plant or animal

freshwater water that is found in streams, rivers, and lakes. Fresh water does not contain salt

grasslands areas where a lot of grass grows, but few trees and shrubs

habitats places in which animals and plants make their homes

hatch to break out of an egg

inject to push a liquid into the body

ligaments stretchy bands of tissue that connect bones

limbs arms or legs

mainland the main area of land near an island

mammals animals that give birth to babies and feed them with milk from their bodies

marshes areas of land that are often covered in water

nerves tiny fibers in the body that send messages around it

predators animals that hunt and eat other animals

prehistoric describes a time before people began to record things, or write them down

prey animals that are hunted and eaten by other animals

rain forest a forest that has a lot of rain

species a group of living creatures that have similar characteristics and can breed with each other

sub-Saharan an area below the Sahara, a large desert in Africa

suffocating stopping from breathing

swamps watery areas with many plants

vibrations movements that can be felt

vital organs important body parts that an animal needs to survive

FIND OUT MORE

Books

Holmes, Parker. *Pythons on the Hunt* (Predators). Lerner Publishing, 2018.

Messner, Kate. *Tracking Pythons: The Quest to Catch an Invasive Predator and Save an Ecosystem.* Lerner Publishing, 2020.

Taylor, Barbara and Mark O'Shea. *The Ultimate Book of Snakes and Reptiles.* Armadillo, 2022.

Websites

Learn more fascinating facts about pythons and other big snakes at:
https://easyscienceforkids.com/all-about-pythons

Find out more about snakes at:
https://kids.britannica.com/kids/article/snake/353785

Discover more about the amazing anaconda at:
www.natgeokids.com/uk/discover/animals/reptiles /anaconda-facts

Publisher's note to educators and parents:
All the websites featured above have been carefully reviewed to ensure that they are suitable for students. However, many websites change often, and we cannot guarantee that a site's future contents will continue to meet our high standards of educational value. Please be advised that students should be closely monitored whenever they access the Internet.

INDEX

About the Author

Katherine Eason has written many books about animals and their environments. In writing this book, she has discovered that big snakes are amazing predators that deserve our respect and protection.